Preface to the First Editio

For over forty years members of the C
footpaths of Gower, both independent.,
regular programme of weekly guided walks. The protection anu ᴄᴏɪ-
servation of the local public footpath network has always been one of
our principal activities. Although the tide has now turned in our favour,
with increased concern shown by public authorities and more general
appreciation of the natural environment, there are still many improve-
ments to be made.

In 1960 I had the pleasure of working with Stephen Lee, our redoubt-
able first Footpaths Officer, on the Society's original footpaths book
Ten Walks in Gower, but this has long been out of print and is indeed
something of a collector's item.

The need for a new book of walks has been apparent for some time
and the Society has been urged to put its knowledge of the footpaths
(or some of them) into print. I am delighted that our dedicated Committee Member and experienced walker Ruth Ridge (ably supported
behind the scenes by her husband, Malcolm) has now combined her
excellent drawings and clear descriptions to create *Gower Walks* on behalf
of the Gower Society. It will tempt both new and seasoned walkers alike
to venture away from the busy tarmac to enjoy "real" Gower, which
still lies just behind the roadside hedgerows.

Bernard Morris
President (1990-1993),
The Gower Society.

Note on the Second Edition

For this new edition of *Gower Walks*, all the walks have been checked
and updated by the author, Gower Society committee members and
friends. In many cases it has been necessary to redraft text and maps to
clarify minor, but otherwise confusing, changes since the first edition.
Any errors remaining are those of the author.

Ruth Ridge, 1999

3

Introduction

"Gower", wrote Dylan Thomas to a friend "is one of the loveliest sea-coast stretches in the whole of Britain, and some of its tiny villages are as obscure, as little inhabited and as lovely as they were a hundred years ago".

Dylan, as a boy, often ventured west from his "ugly, lovely town" of Swansea, past bays "almost too lovely to look at" to that "sea-worm of rock pointing into the channel." Once, he was trapped on Worms Head by the incoming tide and had to walk the eighteen miles back to Swansea by moonlight.

Walking is the only way to see Gower. The traveller in his car cannot know the delicate perfume of the dune rose, the rich melody of the blackcap, the silent mystery of the standing stones. The heart of Gower is open to those who come on foot. You can listen to its secrets and feel the rhythm of its seasons, share its wild places and its places of calm beauty. You can accept Dylan's invitation to "come and see it with me. We shall both utter words of maudlin wonder, and swoon away on the blasted heath".

Gower Walks gives the walker – whether visitor or local resident – clear and concise instructions for thirteen walks that illustrate the immense variety of scenery to be enjoyed within the small compass of peninsular Gower, the first designated Area of Outstanding Natural Beauty in Britain.

The times given for the walks are, of necessity, very approximate, but assume a gentle pace rather than a route march. Distances are given in kilometres and miles at the beginning of each walk, but the descriptions give approximate distances in metres. The maps vary slightly in scale, so check sub-sections against the main map for each walk.

While none of the walks is particularly rough or difficult, strong shoes or boots are advisable, and waterproof clothing is a useful precaution. Be prepared, of course, for mud and encroaching brambles. Binoculars and a hand-lens or magnifying glass can add enormously to the pleasure of what you see. Refreshment is not always easily obtainable, so a picnic or snack can be very welcome. Dogs should be kept on a lead, since farmland, cliffs and common land will be grazed throughout the year by sheep, ponies and cattle. Close all gates and respect the country code. If public transport is used, check the times of the return buses, and if you come by car, always park with care and with consideration for residents and other road users.

4

Virtually all the walks described are on established public rights of way, though occasionally green lanes, frequently used though not formally recognised, are used.

At the end of the book, you will find a list of suggested further reading that will add even more to your understanding and appreciation of this land of Gower.

The spelling of place-names in Gower can be problematic. Some have both English and Welsh versions and some are English corruptions of original Welsh names. Signposts and maps are sometimes inconsistent. As a general rule, we have been guided by the spellings used in the Ordnance Survey, and where they use more than one spelling, we have used what seems the most common version. With names of farms and houses, we have used the spelling that appears on the building itself, even if that differs from the Ordnance Survey's version.

All the paths were surveyed for the book in 1990 and 1991 and again in 1998/99. Over a period of time, changes are bound to occur: stiles may be replaced, gates renovated, fences take the place of hedges. Irrespective of such minor alterations, however, the maps and instructions should be sufficiently clear to keep you on the right path.

Thanks are due to the late David Gillett and Isobel Thomas (former Footpath Officers of the Gower Society) and to Bernard Morris (Publications Officer of the Gower Society) for their help in preparing this book.

Acknowledgements are also due to J. M. Dent and Sons Ltd. for permission to quote extracts from *Dylan Thomas: The Collected Letters*, edited by Paul Ferris.

Ruth Ridge

The following Ordnance Survey maps will be useful:

Landranger No. 159 Swansea and Gower (1:50,000)
Outdoor Leisure Map No. 10 Gower (1:25,000)

5

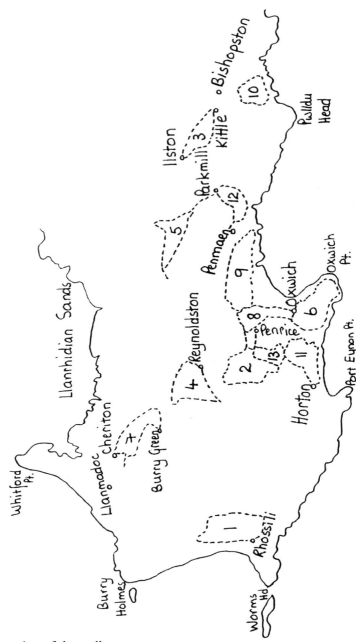

Location of the walks

List of Walks

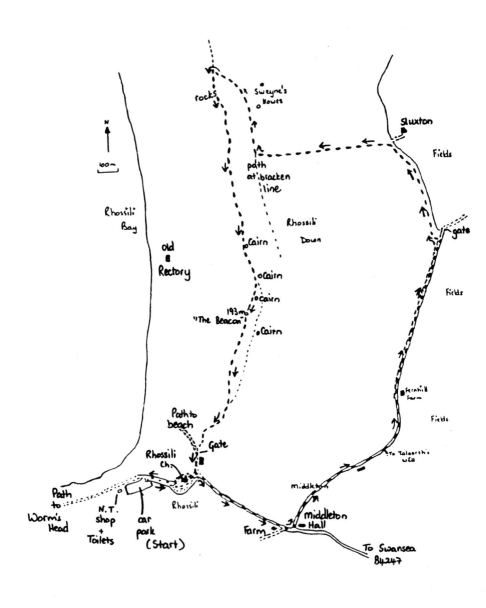

N

100m

rocks

Sweyne's
Howes

Sluxton

Fields

path
at bracken
line

Rhossili
Bay

Old
Rectory

Rhossili
Down

o Cairn

gate

o Cairn

Fields

o Cairn

193m
"The Beacon"

o Cairn

Fernhill
Farm

Fields

Path to
beach

Gate

To Talgarth's
Well

Rhossili
Ch.

middkton

Path
to
Worm's
Head

N.T.
shop
+
Toilets

car
park
(Start)

Rhossili

middleton
Hall

Farm

To Swansea
B4247

Walk 1, general map

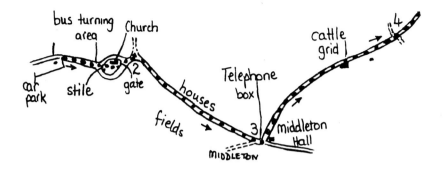

1. Rhossili, Middleton and Rhossili Down

Length: 7 km (4.5 miles)   *Time: 3 hrs*

1. Start from the car park at Rhossili (Grid ref: 416878) and walk up through the village towards Rhossili Church. At the bus-turning area, on L., go behind the house and climb steps into the churchyard. As the gravestones testify, many villagers lived to a ripe old age. The church is dedicated to St. Mary the Virgin, and is probably 13th century in origin. There is late Norman dog-tooth moulding around the doorway, and inside the church is a memorial to Petty Officer Evans who was born in the parish and died with Capt. Scott at the S. Pole. The original church was besanded with the rest of the village on the Warren below.

2. Leave the churchyard by the other gate, and continue on the main road, following the R.-hand bend ahead. Walk along this road with houses on the L. and fine views to the R. over the fields to Worms Head. In 400m, Rhossili merges into Middleton.

3. Take the lane L., between the telephone box and Middleton Hall, soon going uphill with houses on each side. Pass the old village school and go over the cattle grid to reach Rhossili Down (National Trust). On the side of the 2nd house on the R. (Middleton Hall Cottage), a plaque indicates Petty Officer Evans' birthplace.

9

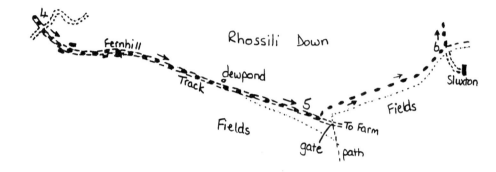

4. Keep ahead on the track (now rougher) along the lower edge of the Down. Passing a ruin on the R. and a dewpond on the L., the view in front extends to Hardings Down, Llangennith, Loughor Estuary and Pembrey, and south to the Bristol Channel and Devon. Milkwort and violet are common here; look for stonechat and linnet.

5. Continue almost to the bottom of the track, and just before the gate, turn L. and cross the narrow ditch onto the moor. Then swing R. to follow the rough path between the telegraph poles and the fence. This stretch involves crossing small streams running off the hill (strategically placed stones help). It can be damp in places, but the path is drier nearer the fence (gorse, tormentil, marsh lousewort and sundew).

10

Sluxton :6 → - - - - - - - -

Rhossili
Down

path

Sweyne
Howes

Rhossili

Rhossili Bay

rocks

8

path

6. By an unused and overgrown entrance gate to Sluxton Farm, turn L. and follow the rather indistinct tractor tracks uphill. Turn R. on reaching the bracken line (where the ground steepens) and follow the clearly visible path heading for a small summit col (heather, bilberry, cotton grass; wheatear, meadow pipit, skylark, buzzard and kestrel).

7. As the path climbs, take a detour down to the R. to the two grassy areas amongst the heather. Here are two Neolithic tombs – the Sweyne Howes (or Swine Houses), over 4,000 years old. Of the two, the N. one is better preserved. From R. to L. you see the high ground of Cefn Bryn, Hardings Down and Llanmadoc Hill.

8. Climbing on up, turn L. onto the summit path with a view across Rhossili Bay to Worms Head, while below are remains of a war-time radar station.

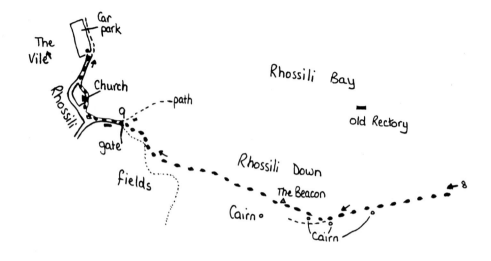

8. (**continued**) Follow this path S. along the top of Rhossili Down. Pass two Bronze Age cairns on the L., then take the R-hand path leading up to The Beacon (Trig. Point at 193m), with another cairn on the L. Burry Holmes now comes into view at the R. end of the Bay. Go ahead and the path descends to Rhossili. If conditions favour take-off, you will see hang gliders here. As the path descends, if it is low tide, you can see the ribs of the "Helvetia" on the sands – wrecked in 1887. Beyond the village, the medieval strip field system the 'Vile' (= 'Field'), can be seen.

9. At the base of the slope go through the swing gate and up the track, turning R. to take the path that passes to the R. of the church-yard wall. Emerge onto the road and return to the car park.

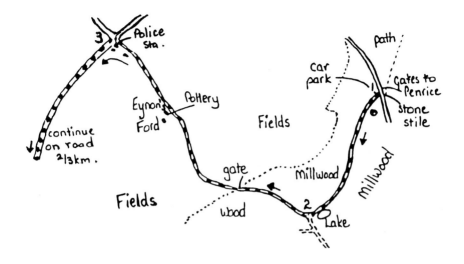

2. Millwood, Eynon's Ford and Berry Wood

Length: 7.5 km (5 miles)   *Time: 2.5 hrs*

This walk starts at "Pennyhitch", on the Penrice road, at the small car park by Millwood (Grid ref: 494883).

1. Go through the gate into Millwood and follow the wide gravel path until you reach the small lake (mallard, jay, grey wagtail, warblers).

2. At the end of the lake, take the first path on the R., leading uphill and eventually out of the wood beside a wooden gate. Follow the wide stony track uphill to Eynon's Ford, passing fields on the L. There is a pottery in the first house.

3. Turn L. onto the main road beside the Police House (Danger – traffic can be fast). Continue until you reach the entrance to Stouthall, the 18th century residence of the Lucas family, and more recently leased as a field study centre. Cross the road here and go through the gate into the field.

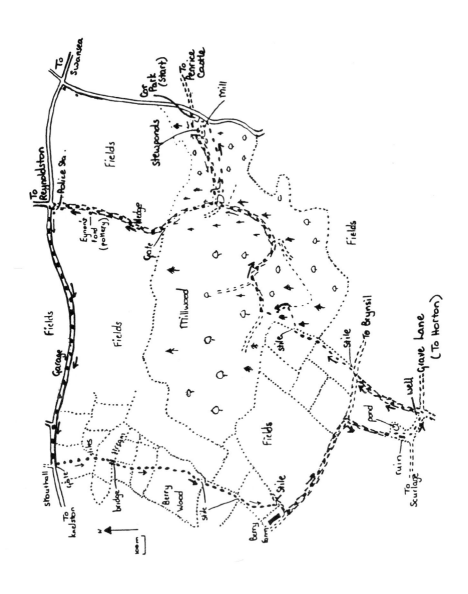

Walk 2, general map

14

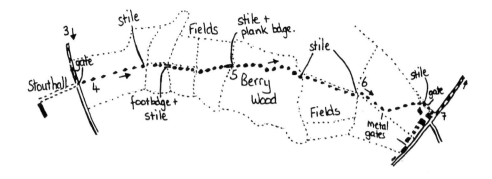

4. Follow the raised remains of an old field boundary across the fields, crossing over the stiles. Descend to a wooden bridge and over a stile to follow the L.-hand hedge through the marshy fields (stile), heading for the Glamorgan Wildlife Trust's sign, by a stile (buzzard, kestrel, lapwing).

5. Enter Berry Wood over the stile and then a rough plank bridge. The path winds through the wood, and is not always clear. Three-quarters of the way through the wood, you will cross a narrow ditch with plank bridge. Leave the wood over a stile and go up the field, keeping the hedge and ditch on your L.

6. Cross the stile, and go up the next field with the hedge on the R. this time. Half-way up the field (by metal gates) go diagonally across the field, aiming for the top L. corner, to the L. of the farm buildings. Cross the stile and turn R. onto a lane that passes the farm on your R.

15

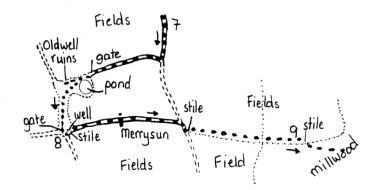

7.   At the T-junction in 50m, turn L. and follow the track for 650m.
Turn R. and go along the green lane between the hedges. Emerge onto
a wide green area with a pond on the L. (broad leaved pondweed,
water crowfoot and moorhen). This is the site of the hamlet of Oldwell
– note ruins on the R. Swing L. and follow the path uphill. At the
fence at the top you may be able to see the remains of the old well near
the stile.

8.   Turn L. and follow the track that passes an isolated cottage known
as Merry Sun. At the T-junction, turn R. and in 10m, turn L. over a
stile. Go ahead down the field (look for field pansy, corn spurrey) and
ahead in the next field with the wood now on your R.

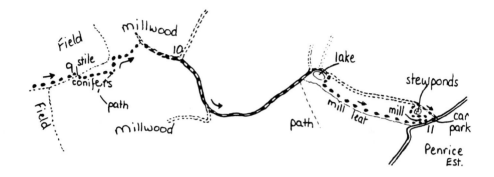

9. Half-way down the field cross stile into wood on R. The path here is not always clear. Head leftish through the conifers and pick up a path (turn L. onto it) marked with blue posts, beyond the conifers. Emerging onto a broad green track, turn R. and follow it until you meet a T-junction.

10. Turn R. here onto a wide track and continue ahead. At the next track junction, turn L. on the wide gravel track that runs downhill to the lake. Go three-quarters of the way round the lake, keeping it on your R., and take the narrow path (on R.) by the rhododendron bushes that then goes L. to follow the old mill-leat through the wood. You emerge at the ruins of the old Penrice corn-mill. Note the mill stone.

11. Swing to the L. past the mill and walk round the excavated remains of Penrice Castle stewponds, where fish were farmed for the table. To reach the car, take the path at the far L. of the stewponds. In 10m, turn R. and follow the wide track for 50m until you pass out of the wood at the gate by the car park.

17

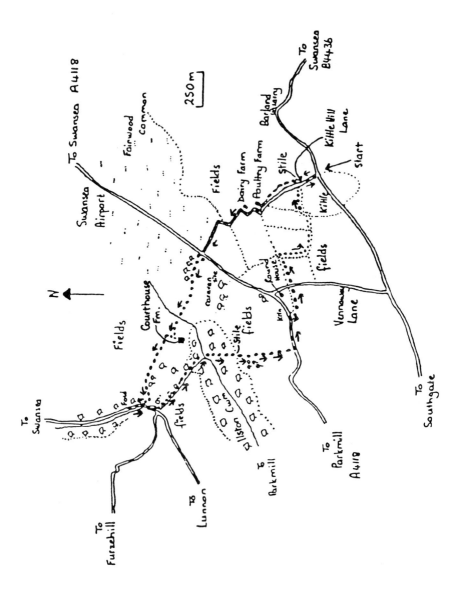

Walk 3, general map

18

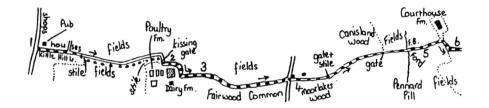

3. Kittle and Ilston

Length: 5.5 km (3.5 miles)   *Time: 2 hrs*

1. Starting from the village green in Kittle (Grid ref: 574893), walk along Kittle Hill Lane, beside the Beaufort Arms, passing bungalows on each side. Where the lane narrows, cross the stile on the R-hand side and go ahead over further stiles, following the line of the lane.

2. Exit through the kissing-gate by the Kittle Poultry Farm and continue on the road R., past the Kittle Hill Farm. Buzzards are often seen here.

3. Road continues onto Fairwood Common, meeting the main Swansea-Rhossili road (A4118) at a T-junction. To the R. is Swansea Airport. Cross over the main road and enter the broad track, passing a house on the L.

4. The woodland on the R. is Moorlakes Wood – it is damp woodland, largely oak, supporting many birds. Look out for violets, primrose, lesser celandine, wood oxalis, dog's mercury, wood anemone and bluebell. The track passes over a stile beside a gate; water draining off the high banks can make it damp here. Gently descend through a metal gate to a small stream. This can be forded in dry weather, or crossed on the footbridge to the L. Look for buzzards.

5. Continue on the high-banked track uphill, which curves L. to Courthouse Farm. Before reaching the farmyard, turn R. along the track, keeping the wall and hedge on L. Good views over the valley towards Cannisland Wood.

19

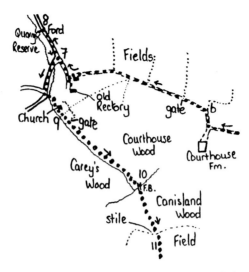

6.   At the end of wall, turn L. along a grassy path between stunted hawthorns. Pass ahead over the stile into a banked lane (may be muddy). In season, honeysuckle, red campion, wild strawberry and cuckoo flower thrive here. Descend to Ilston village, entering the village with the white-gated Old Rectory on your L. Turn sharp R. with horse chestnuts over the wall on L., and go ahead, passing a cottage on R. beside a gate. Pass through to reach the road through the village.

7.   At junction, turn R. (stream on L.). About 50m on L., across a ford, is the Glamorgan Wildlife Trust's Ilston Quarry Reserve. Trees beside the road usually have tits, treecreeper and nuthatch.

8.   Retrace your steps to the village with houses on the R. and the stream (snowdrops on bank) on the L. Cross the stream to enter the churchyard. The church is dedicated to St. Illtyd and probably dates, in its present form, from the late Middle Ages. The ancient yew may be 600 years old. Note some interesting and beautifully engraved memorial stones.

9.   Take the path through the churchyard with the stream on the R. and enter Carey's Wood by the black gate. The path follows the stream, which in dry weather may flow underground in places. Debris in the bushes will indicate the heights it can reach in wet weather! On the L. you pass the curved-wall remains of a limekiln with evidence of nearby quarry workings.

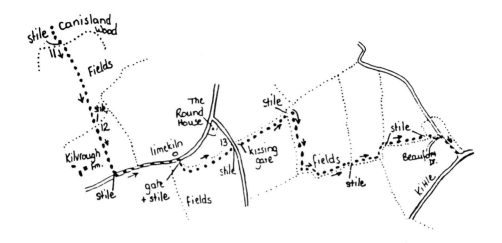

10. Cross a tributary stream on a concrete bridge. Do not turn R. to follow the path down the valley (which leads to Parkmill), but go ahead uphill on a path rising between the trees. This leads up and out of the wood over a stile.

11. Go straight ahead up the cleft in the field, keeping L. of a group of 4 trees. Continue ahead across the field aiming for a stile.

12. Cross over stile, and go ahead down the field to leave it over another stile onto the road. Turn L. (CARE!) and follow it uphill for about 250m. A well-restored limekiln is seen on the L. Opposite this, cross over stone stile beside gate into a field. Follow L.-hand hedge ahead for approx. 25m and then round R. following hedge to exit field over stile.

13. Pass over (Beware, traffic!) and cross road to kissing gate opposite. Go through and follow the L.-hand hedge to stile into next field. Turn R. and follow hedge round field to exit over a stile in far corner. Go ahead following R.-hand hedge to leave field over a stile by a housing estate. Cross this stile, and go ahead following the hedge to leave over another stile. Follow the narrow path out onto Beaufort Drive. 15m ahead is Kittle Hill Lane where you turn R. to return to the village green.

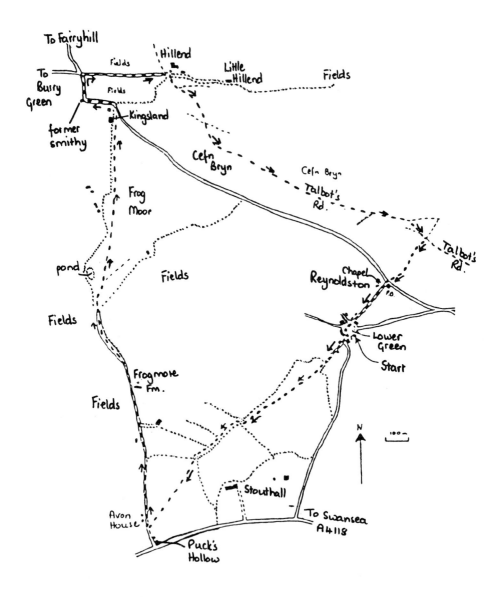

Walk 4, general map

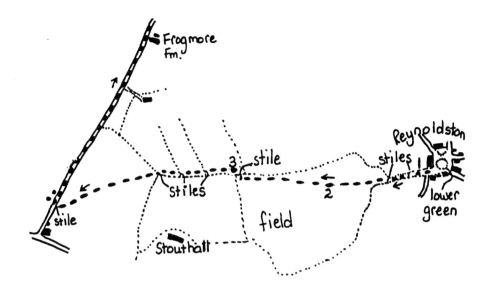

4. Reynoldston, Knelston, Frogmoor and Cefn Bryn

Length: 5 km (3 miles)   *Time: 2.5 hrs*

1. At the S.E. corner of the lower green in Reynoldston (Grid ref: 479899), take the track marked "Knelston 1.6km" with a stream on your R. Soon you cross a stile and then the stream (monkey flower). Go ahead over the next stile into a field.

2. The large house now seen to the L. is Stouthall (see Walk 2). Head across the field to the R.-hand corner. The view to the R. takes in Rhossili and Hardings Down plus Llanmadoc Hill.

3. Just before the gate, cross the stile over the R.-hand fence to the adjoining field. Keep L. along the edge and stream, crossing over the 3 stiles ahead (buzzard, rook, lapwing). Go diagonally across this large field to the wooden stile to the L. of the 4th telegraph pole. Turn R. at Avon House up the metalled lane (common fleabane, blackthorn, honeysuckle, water mint).

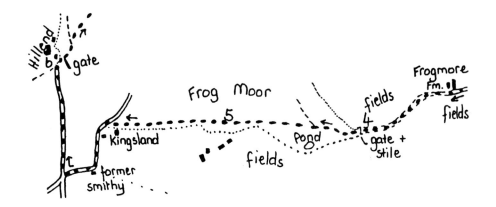

4. 0.5 km past Frogmore* Farm, cross one of the Gower Society's Jubilee stiles beside a gate where the metalled track ends. Continue across Frogmoor (common land) following a broad grassy track that swings R. and then L. across the lower part of the moor. Ignore the R.-hand path leading up to the cottage. Your route follows a definable path that runs on a stony base, in parts raised slightly above the surroundings. Continue on path passing an iris-rich pond on your L. (also marsh St. John's wort, heather, bell heather, gorse). Path narrows and then widens; ignore house and stile on L.

5. Pass, some distance away, four cottages on your L. Head towards two cottages (hamlet is Kingsland) and keep them close to your L. Cross stile (note well on L.) and reach road where you turn L. downhill to pass a house on your L. As you round the R.-hand bend note on the L. a ruined building which was once a smithy. At the cross-roads, turn R. uphill, following a lane.

* See page 5 for explanation of place name variations.

24

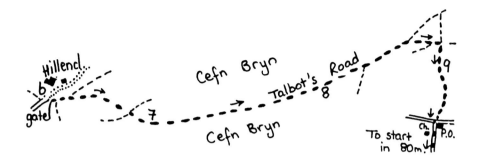

6. When you reach Hillend, turn R. onto a marked bridleway that rises on bracken-covered slopes. Pass through the gate and climb up the slopes of Cefn Bryn. 150m uphill take the R. fork under the wires and continue steeply up. There are views back over the Loughor Estuary, Pembrey, and the Black Mountains.

7. Continue uphill and go ahead at the cross-roads of tracks on the broad grassy track. This track is called Talbot's Road and was built as a carriage-way by the Talbot family of Penrice in the 19th century. Aim for the line of poles crossing the track and ignore all side paths.

8. Pass under the overhead wires, ignore the next R. turn, but take the R.-hand fork at the Y-junction. The path continues uphill, bearing slightly L. 100m further on. At the crossroads of tracks in 10m, turn R. onto a broad track (you will know that you are in the correct place because there are stone-coloured B.T. manhole covers beside the path in 8m) that soon drops downhill to Reynoldston.

9. There is a good view of Stouthall ahead with Lundy Island (far out in the Bristol Channel) beyond it on the horizon. Descend to the road, cross to the Post Office, and go down the road to its R. to reach the start of the walk at the lower green.

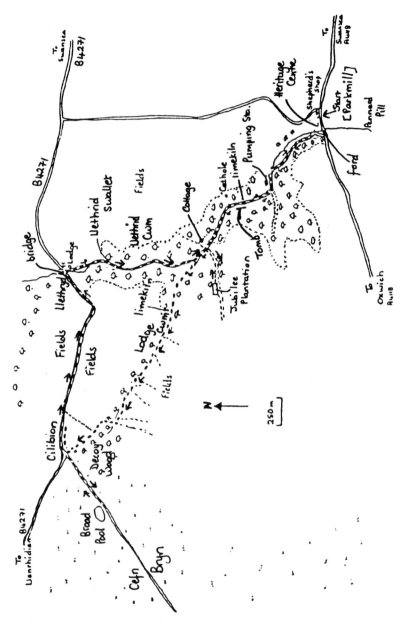

Walk 5, general map

26

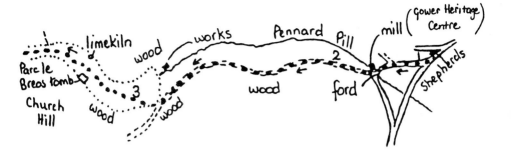

5. Parkmill, Lodge Cwm and Llethrid Cwm

Length: 10 km (6 miles)   *Time: 3-3.5 hrs*

1. Start from the shop in the village of Parkmill (Grid ref: 544892) and walk along the lane, past cottages on R., towards the Mill buildings. The water-powered mill has been a cornmill, and more recently, a sawmill. Now it is the Gower Heritage Centre housing craft sales and a museum. You can still see the mill operating. Cross the stream (Pennard Pill) on the footbridge and turn R. up tarmac lane marked Parc-le-Breos (private road). Parc-le-Breos was originally a hunting estate of the Norman le Breos family, Lords of Gower between 1203 and 1320.

2. Follow this lane with wood on L. (primrose, bluebell, wood anemone, wild garlic, dog's mercury). The field on R. has clumps of marsh marigold and cuckoo flower, and – if you are lucky – kingfishers may be glimpsed on the stream. Turn R. after the Welsh Water pumping station (which pumps water to a reservoir on the top of Cefn Bryn) and go through gate into Green Cwm (Llethrid Cwm) – the stream is now flowing underground.

3. Continue on wide track through grassy valley until you reach on L., Parc-le-Breos Tomb (Giants Grave), dating from approx. 3,500 BC – a megalithic, chambered, long barrow. Opposite it, is a restored limekiln. About 100m further on, is a steep R. path leading up to Cathole Cave – in which have been found prehistoric (late Ice Age) human and animal remains. Look out for buzzard, jay, nuthatch, treecreeper, goldcrest and tits.

4. Just past Green Cwm Cottage (on R.), turn L. for 200m diversion to see the Gower Society Jubilee plantation of 300 broad-leaved lime trees and seat. Return to crossroads and turn L. In 100m, at R.H.-bend, take less distinct L.-band path through wood and then up a wooded valley (cleared on R.H. side). Limestone outcrops on the R. are obscured by undergrowth (silverweed, wood spurge, meadowsweet, kestrel, blackcap, goldfinch).

5. 40m past a limekiln on R., cross the stile and go ahead over field to 2nd stile. Cross this, and then go through next small (30m) copse, leaving it at a 3rd stile – note the ruin of Lodge Farm on R. of fence (stiles may be dilapidated). The next stile is beside a large stone gatepost.

6. Go ahead and in 20m turn down a wide high-banked track. Cross the stream and take the stile on L. into the field. The path follows the fence by Decoy Wood and the original deep lane, on the L. Cross stile in fence into next field, and leave this field by a wooden stile to R. of house. This is in the hamlet of Cilibion.

7. Turn L. and head for road which climbs up over Cefn Bryn. Follow this for 700m until you reach Broad Pool on R. This was Glamorgan Wildlife Trust's first reserve in 1962. Good for dragonflies, amphibians, etc.

8. Return to Cilibion and continue on main road (B4271) towards Swansea [Extreme care – this stretch can be dangerous] (passing the garage on R.) for about 2km, to the scattered buildings of Llethryd*. After the road dips to cross the stream by a bridge, take the track to the R. past the restored Lodge. Cross over the stile, and continue on gravel track ahead. This valley (Llethrid Cwm) contains the Pennard Pill, flowing underground for much of its length. 200m along on the L., you will see the entrance to Llethrid Swallet – a huge limestone cave – only for experienced cavers. In the same clearing are two charcoal burning kilns (which may be hot) and associated wood-stores. These woods contain a large variety of birds.

9. Continue on the track and you will rejoin your original path just before the crossroads and Green Cwm Cottage (see section 4). Retrace your steps to Parkmill.

*See page 5 for explanation of place-name variations.

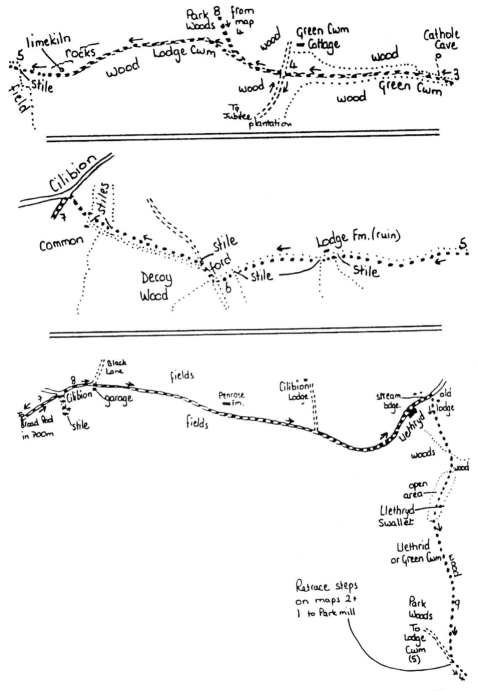

limekiln
rocks
5
Park 8 from
Woods map
4
Green Cwm
Cottage
Cathole
Cave
P
stile
field
wood
Lodge Cwm
wood
wood
4
wood
3
wood
wood
Green Cwm
To
Jubilee plantation

Cilibion
7
stiles
Common
stile
ford
Decoy
Wood
6
stile
stile
Lodge Fm. (ruin)
stile
5

Black
Lane
fields
8
Cilibion
garage
Penrose
fm.
Cilibion
Lodge
stream
bdge.
old
lodge
7
To
Broad Pool
in 700m
stile
fields
Llethryd
woods
open
area
wood
Llethryd
Swallet
Llethrid
or Green Cwm
Retrace steps
on maps 2 +
1 to Park mill
Park
Woods
To
Lodge
Cwm
(5)
wood
9

29

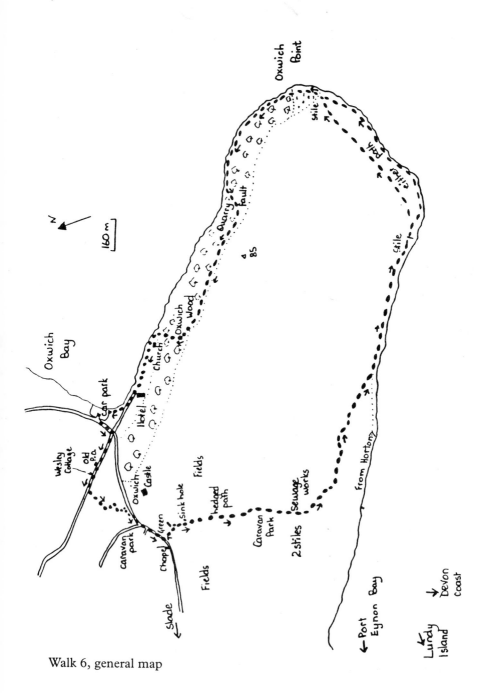

Walk 6, general map

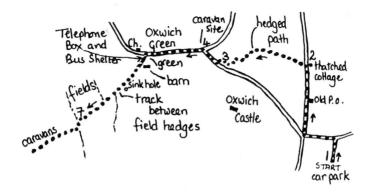

6.   Oxwich, Oxwich Green and Oxwich Point

Length: 8 km (5 miles)   *Time: 3 hrs*

1.   Start from the car park at Oxwich beach (Grid ref: 502865). Turn L. out of the car park, and R. at crossroads. Follow road through village, passing (on your R.) old Post Office (now a craft shop) and thatched cottage where John Wesley is reputed to have preached.

2.   Turn L. (signposted Oxwich Green) before next thatched cottage on R., up gated track (marked Village Hall) for 30m. Continue uphill on much narrower hedged path for 300m. Views back across Oxwich Bay on L.

3.   At top of path, good view of Oxwich Castle ruins. Turn R. and walk up road. Note wall pennywort and ivy-leaved toadflax on wall on R.

4.   Bend L. at junction and walk into Oxwich Green village, passing caravan site entrance on R.

5.   Pass the small green and turn L. at the telephone box and bus shelter (before reaching the former Methodist Chapel on R.). Go ahead on track, to the R. of renovated barn complex, behind which were the ruins of an old – reputedly 16th century – farmhouse.

6.   Continue on track (may be damp), passing sink hole beneath syca-more on L. after 50m. Track becomes drier (lesser celandine, primrose, wild garlic, bluebell; tortoiseshell, red admiral, and speckled wood butterflies). Views to R. of Port Eynon Bay and across to Devon and Lundy Island, distant in the Bristol Channel.

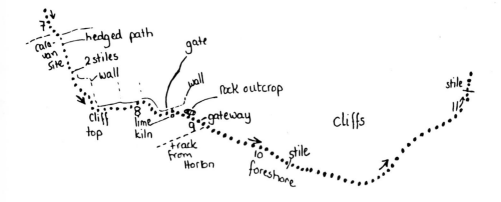

7. Pass caravan site (on your R.) and cross two stiles onto cliff pasture land. Follow L.-hand wall round onto cliff-top and continue L. along cliff-top.

8. Cross metal gate and go ahead through wooden gate to turn immediately R. down a valley passing below a rock outcrop on L. (common scurvy-grass). Follow rocky path downhill entering primrose-strewn pasture through gateway with large stone gatepost (cowslip, milkwort, gorse, spring squill, early purple orchid, violets, hemp agrimony, tormentil, wood sage).

9. Ahead is Lucas's Bay. Path joins from R. coming from Horton across the fields. Note the wave-cut platform of the foreshore, especially visible at low tide (oystercatchers, turnstones) with good pools for crabbers.

10. Continue ahead above the shore – look out for raven, jackdaw, buzzard, linnet, stonechat, meadow pipit, rock pipit, house martin, and hunting peregrine. Go ahead at gate noting rock arch above pool on shore.

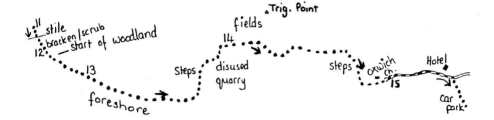

11. Further round Oxwich Point at the wooden stile leading into Oxwich National Nature Reserve, look for auks, fulmar, cormorant, shag, gannet and terns out at sea.

12. Path leads through bracken for about 75m into wood. Views across Oxwich Bay to Cefn Bryn, Nicholaston, and Penmaen, and further round to Whiteshell Point beyond Caswell Bay and to Aberthaw (60 km east) in the distance.

13. Path undulates in wood before swinging uphill away from foreshore (wood oxalis, bluebell, wild strawberry, wild garlic). View towards old and new Penrice Castles across bay. Steps and a protective wooden barrier lead around a disused quarry on R. with beech trees (Dangerous!). A fault line is seen higher up on the L. of the path; path eventually levels out beside wire fence on L.

14. Trig. Point (85m) is visible across the field on L. Keep ahead on path through top of wood (ignore paths on L.). Turn R. down steep flight (269?) of steps to edge of bay. Swing L. to pass Church of St. Illtyd (Oxwich) hidden in trees on L. Rookery in trees above. Church dates from 13th century and is worth a visit. There are two 14th century memorials.

15. Continue on lane towards Oxwich Bay Hotel (on L.). Turn R. into car park at top of beach.

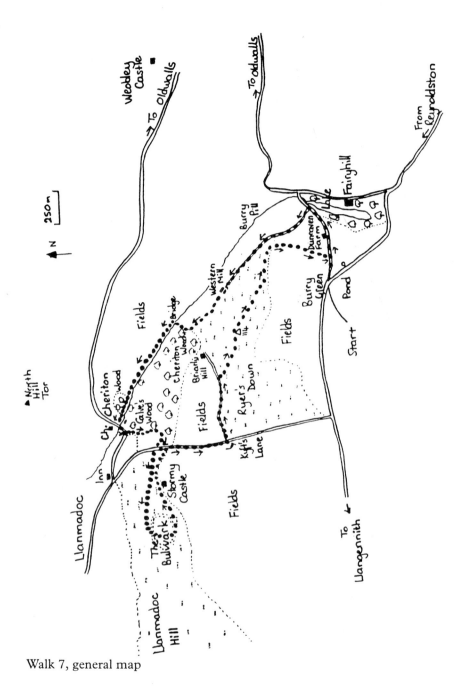

Walk 7, general map

34

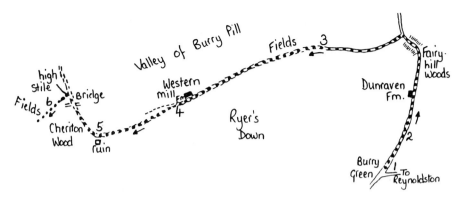

7. Burry Green, Cheriton and Ryer's Down

Length: 6 or 7.5 km (4 or 5 miles)   *Time: 2 hrs (or 2.5 hrs)*

1. This walk starts at the green in Burry Green (Grid ref: 463914). Note the pond (water crowfoot, watermint, etc.), and the Tudor-style house called Burry Cottage. This was a former home of a Society past-President (Sidney Heath).

2. Take road E. towards Stembridge, passing on L., Dunraven Farm. Soon, on the R., are Fairyhill woods, and road descends through a rock cutting, past a disused quarry on L. Half-way down the hill, at a bend, take farm track on L. leading along the contour of the hill with fields on R.

3. Track opens out at the foot of Ryer's Down. Continue, with bracken-covered Down on L. and fence and later, field walls on R. There are wide views over the valley of the Burry Pill. Track becomes grassy as you pass isolated Western Mill Farm on R. (2 millstones in wall).

4. Just beyond Western Mill Farm, keep on the grass path and continue to woodland. Rhododendrons are becoming invasive on L., but are being tackled by the National Trust. The path passes an enclosed overgrown ruin on L. before entering the trees.

5. Continue downhill, forking to the R. on the (sometimes muddy) track below beech trees to the stream (Burry Pill). Cross the stream on the old three-arched bridge and pass over the L.-hand high wooden stile into a field.

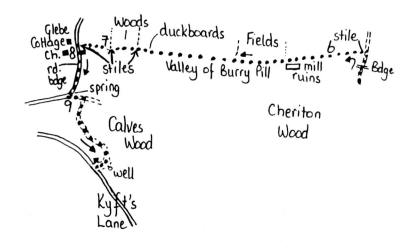

6.   Keep on (crossing stiles) along the lower edge of the fields, with the stream on L., until you reach the wood. Beside the fence there is duck-boarding to help cross a muddy section. Cross the stile and follow the path through the short stretch of wood (wood anemone, bluebell, early purple orchid, lesser celandine, red campion, primrose).

7.   Leave wood over stile and cross the field, keeping to the L.-hand edge. Cross over the stone stile in the wall into the road opposite Cheriton Church (dedicated to St. Cadoc). Glebe Cottage (on the R. of the church) has a rare octagonal medieval chimney. The 14th century church is worth a visit – 3rd grave on L. is that of Freud's biographer, Dr Ernest Jones.

8.   Take the road L. downhill, crossing the stream, and at the bend **either**: continue along the road to the Britannia Inn (which does pub food) and then turn sharp L. uphill

9.   **or**: Take the upper of two drives on the L. (running back on the road) and follow the track steeply uphill to the L. of Hillside, through the wood until it opens out at the top of the wood by a house and triangle of grass (with a well on L.). Turn L. onto road and go uphill, following No. 10 below, unless you take a detour to the Bulwark.

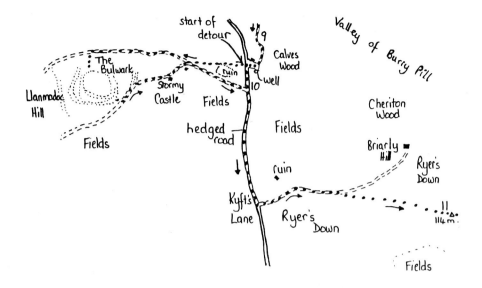

Detour to the Bulwark: Cross road, taking grass path through the bracken ahead; pass ruins and Stormy Castle on your L. Pick up stony track winding round Llanmadoc Hill and then climb up to the L. to reach the well-preserved complex of ramparts and ditches of an Iron Age Hill Fort – the Bulwark. The inner enclosure of nearly 1 hectare has an entrance to the east, and was later enlarged and strengthened. There are over a dozen Bronze-Age cairns along the ridge. Views extend across the Loughor Estuary, to the N. of Swansea, and over S. Gower to Worms Head and Rhossili Down. Return to the road.

10. Continue on the road (Kyft's Lane) for 300m until the fields open onto Ryer's Down. Turn L. onto the stony track and follow this until (after 250m) you strike off R. obliquely uphill – the grass path is clearly seen ahead between the gorse. This lower area may be damp. Head uphill and make for the white Trig. Point (114m) on the top. Views towards Bristol Channel, across Loughor Estuary, and straight ahead to the end of Cefn Bryn.

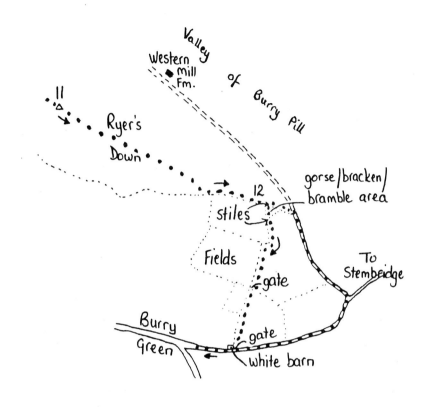

11. Continue past the Trig. Point, and follow path, keeping to a gentle descent towards the field edge on R., where the path meets a broad grass track. Continue steeply downhill until a high wooden stile is seen on R.

12. You can now **either**:
   a. Descend to the valley bottom, turn R. onto the lane leading back to the road; turn R. then for Burry Green **or**
   b. Turn R., cross stile into small area of gorse/bramble/bracken, and then cross 2nd stile to enter a field. Keep to R.-hand hedge and leave field through gate. Go down 2nd field to R.-hand corner gate by white barn. Pass through gate onto road in Burry Green.

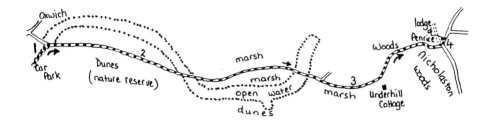

8. Oxwich and Penrice

Length: 6 km (4 miles)   *Time: 2 hrs*

This walk starts from the car park at Oxwich beach (Grid ref: 502865), and involves walking on roads and on public footpaths through the (private) Penrice Estate.

1.   Leave car park, turning R. onto the marsh road. Walk along this road, keeping Oxwich Burrows on the R. This is a National Nature Reserve, supporting many species of orchids and other limestone and dune-loving species such as round-leaved wintergreen, evening primrose, sea holly, rest harrow, red valerian and dewberry.

2.   On the L. is the wetter area of Oxwich Marsh. Bittern have been seen here and osprey, on passage. Buzzards are frequently seen circling, and kestrels hovering. In winter, the open waters attract many species including pochard, tufted duck, shoveler, mallard, little grebe, coot, moorhen, and water rail. Kingfisher, heron and cormorant may be seen. There has been an extensive heronry in Penrice Estate in the past.

3.   Continuing along the road, climb the hill, passing Underhill Cottage on the R., and the walls of Penrice Estate on the L. At the top of the hill are the mock castellations at the entrance to Penrice Estate.

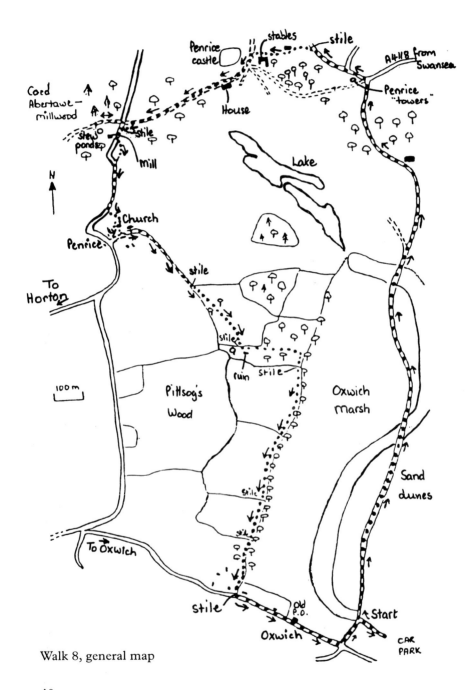

Coed
Abertawe —
millwood

stew
ponds

stile

mill

N

Penrice
castle

stables

stile

A4118 from
Swansea

Penrice
"towers"

House

Lake

Church

Penrice

To
Horton

stile

100 m

Pittsog's

Wood

stile

ruin   stile

Oxwich
Marsh

Sand
dunes

To Oxwich

stile

stile

stile

Start

Oxwich

old
P.O.

CAR
PARK

Walk 8, general map

40

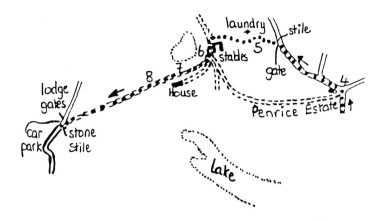

4. Turn L., taking the main road (A4118) towards Port Eynon. After 150m, turn L. into the Estate at signpost over a stone stile set in the wall beside a gate.

5. Cross the field ahead and slightly R. (old laundry on the R.) and follow the yellow-marked posts down the grassy slope to an Estate road. Turn L. onto this road, passing the old stable block.

6. At a meeting of 5 roads/tracks, turn R. to walk past the house. The garden will be on your L. and the ruins of the 13th century Penrice Castle rise up on the R. This, largest of Gower castles, has a stone pigeon house in reasonable condition outside the S.E. wall (probably late 15th century).

7. Looking L. over the garden just before you reach the house, you can see the lake in its beautiful setting. The site of the heronry was in the trees on the R. of the lake. Keep strictly to the path, respecting the owners' privacy.

8. Continue past the house and walk downhill, past the chestnut-leaved oak tree recently planted (July 1998) by the Prince of Wales to commemorate his visit to the Gower Society. Follow the tarmac drive to the gates at the Millwood entrance. Cross over the stone stile in the wall to the L. of the gates. (Here is an alternative car park from which the walk can be started).

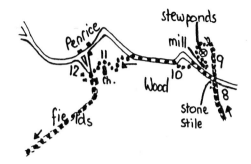

9. (A detour could be made here to visit the Estate stewponds, where fish were farmed for the table, situated in the woods on the opposite side of the road. Nearby are the ruins of the Penrice corn-mill. Enter Coed Abertawe (Millwood) and after about 80m, turn L. to visit the excavated stewponds and the mill. Return to the road.)

10. Go uphill (to the South), following the dog-leg of part of "Penny-hitch", so called, it is said, because having visited the mill, carters could – for a penny fee – hire extra horse-power to get them back up the hill on either side of it! After the metal gate on the L., a track cuts off the bend, and you can regain the road soon after. In 100m, turn L. up a path through the wood. This brings you up into the rear of the Penrice churchyard of St. Andrew's (snowdrops in Spring).

11. The gravestones are worth investigating. Near the path to the S.W. of the church is the grave of a murder victim: "Here lies Mary wife of James Kavanagh of Penmaen, who was murdered by (blank) on 3rd of October 1829 aged 75 years". The large porch may have been used as a school in the past. There are superb views over Oxwich Bay and the dunes.

12. Go out through the gate onto the village green. Turn L. and follow the curving track downhill between the two houses (on the L., views open out over the length of Cefn Bryn).

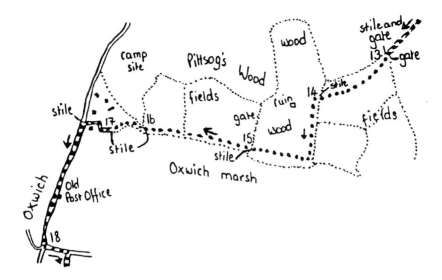

13. Continue straight on and over stile to enter field ahead. Cross the field slightly L. towards a stile in the fence bordering the woodland. Go over stile, turn left and follow the narrow path running down through the wood.

14. The path may be overgrown in places. At the T-junction at the bottom of the wood, turn R., leaving the wood shortly over a stile.

15. Continue ahead across two fields, keeping close to the edge of Oxwich Marsh. The trees here support many birds (jay, tits, warblers, finches). Buzzards are often seen over Pittsog's Wood above the fields.

16. Leave the fields over a small stream crossing a plank bridge and a stile. The path goes straight ahead and is marked by poles across the grassland (private land). Keep to the path at all times. In summer, this grassland supports a fine display of orchids.

17. Pass over the stile and follow the narrow path between two properties. Cross the next stile, (Beware traffic!) turning L. to walk along the single track road through Oxwich village. On the L., you will pass the cottage where John Wesley is believed to have preached from an upstairs window.

18. At the crossroads, turn L., and the car park is 50m along on the R.

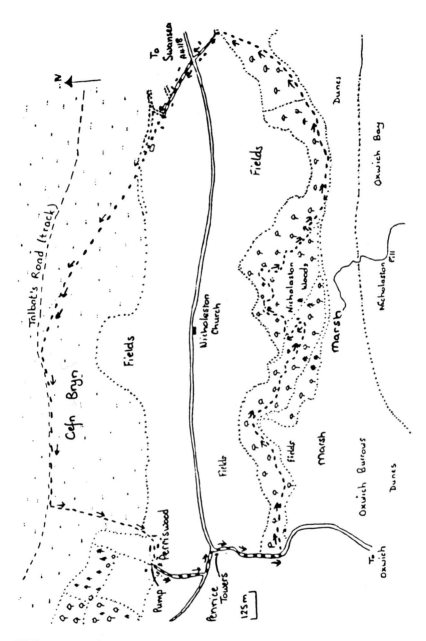

Walk 9, general map

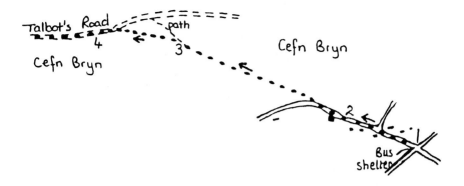

9. Cefn Bryn and Nicholaston Woods

Length: 8 km (5 miles)   *Time: 3 hrs*

1. This walk starts in the village of Nicholaston, at the minor cross-roads on the A4118 (Swansea to Rhossili) road, 0.5km past Penmaen Post Office (Grid ref: 522884).

2. From the bus-shelter, walk uphill on the minor road, passing the castellated building (was Nicholaston House Hotel) on L. Where the road swings left behind the hotel, turn off onto a stony track leading diagonally uphill onto the bracken-covered slopes of Cefn Bryn (skylark, meadow pipit, wheatear).

3. Near the top, take a L.-hand, grassy fork that continues upwards and N.W. until it meets the track running along the top of Cefn Bryn. This is "Talbot's Road", cut in the last century by the Talbot family of Penrice, who liked to ride their carriages along this sandstone ridge, "the back-bone of Gower".

4. Continue N.W. along the broad grassy track. There are superb views S. across Oxwich Bay towards Oxwich Point. On a clear day you will see Lundy Island far to the S.W., the Devon and Somerset coasts, and the Pembrokeshire coast as far as Tenby and Caldey Island.

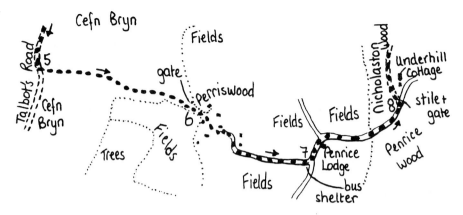

5.   In about 500m, the track dips slightly downhill before beginning
to rise gently again. 200m after it begins to rise, and where the track
bends slightly to the L. before swinging back R., watch out for a broad
grassy path to the L. At this point, the whole panorama of Rhossili
Down and the Downs to the N.W. tip of Gower, come into view. Take
this broad path L., which almost immediately narrows, and go straight
down the southern slopes of Cefn Bryn, to the hamlet of Perriswood.
This section can be rough going, and damp in the lower regions, where
water runs off the hill. Head to the L. of the field stone wall, and continue down until you meet a metal gate onto a track.

6.   Go through the gate and follow the rough track, turning R. onto
the village green, which you cross. (Note the remains of the village pump.)
Leave Perriswood S. on the metalled road which has (on the L.) a
ditch that is slab-lined in places, channelling the water from Cefn Bryn
towards the Penrice Estate. In 300m you reach the main S. Gower road.

7.   Cross the road (Beware, traffic!), turn L. and go 100m to the Penrice
main gates. Turn R. onto the road going downhill towards Oxwich.
Half-way down the hill, turn L. into the broad track running through
Nicholaston Woods. (Oxwich National Nature Reserve.)

8.   Cross the stone stile beside the gate to enter the woods. Birds of
deciduous woodland abound: woodpeckers, tits, warblers, treecreeper,
nuthatch, wren, robin; overhead you may see buzzard, kestrel, raven,
rook, jay, magpie and sparrowhawk. Flowers include bluebell, dog's
mercury, wood anemone, wild strawberry, lesser celandine, ground ivy,
bugle, violets, primrose, wood spurge, wood sorrel, wild garlic.

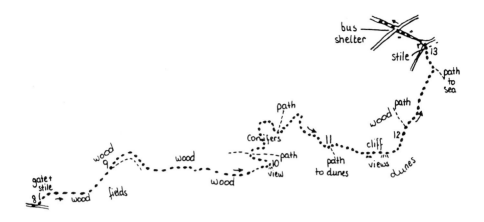

9. Go ahead until the track divides and then take the rougher uphill track. As this eventually levels out, there are views S. over Oxwich Marsh. Look for the dark green bushes of butcher's broom – an unusual plant. The tough green "leaves" are flattened stems; the flowers on the "leaves" are tiny and pale – a red berry forms later.

10. After rounding a limestone bluff, follow the path through conifers. At the crossroads, carry on ahead. After some 150m, the path will begin to descend.

11. Near the bottom of the wood take the L.-hand narrow path (by a rough plank seat) upwards for 5m. Path then bends R. and soon emerges onto a marvellous limestone-backed viewing platform over the sweep of Oxwich Bay, Burrows and Marsh. The small stream meandering out onto the sands is Nicholaston Pill.

12. Continue on the path which descends through the stunted trees on the edge of the cliffs. Rock-roses do well here. Cross the tree-dotted, grassy space and continue on the path opposite, through the trees parallel to the sand dunes. The path leads to a sandy track, by a small stream. Turn L., following the track uphill, with rough steps towards the top.

13. Emerge onto a broad track with a garden hedge on R. Cross the stone stile ahead and swing L. up the road. In about 100m, cross the main S. Gower road (Beware, traffic!) and you are back at the start.

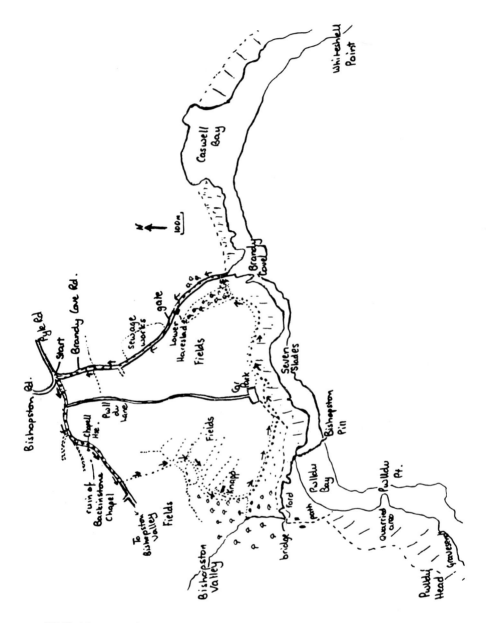

Walk 10, general map

48

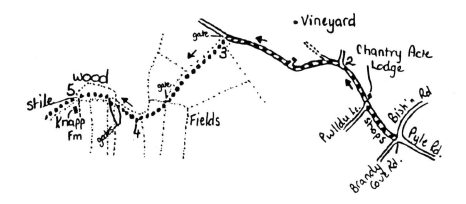

10. Pwlldu and Brandy Cove

Length: 4 km (2.5 miles)   *Time: 1.5 hrs*

1. Start at Pyle Corner in the centre of Bishopston (Grid ref. 580883). Go down Pwlldu Lane, passing shops on L., and after 80m, at L.-hand bend, take lane ahead, with thatched Chantry Acre Lodge on R. (red campion, bluebell, ground ivy).

2. Continue along banked lane past Vineyard. Once past Chapell House on R., look over hedge to see ivy-clad ruin of Backingstone Chapel. 5m past metal gate on L. pass through kissing gate.

3. Go down field keeping hedge on R. to pass through metal kissing gate in R.-hand corner. Head across next field aiming for wide earthy track beneath hawthorns (in line with telegraph pole). Look out for buzzard, kestrel and finches.

4. Go ahead into field, keeping to hedge on R. and pass through kissing gate to continue through a narrow overgrown field. Leave through a further kissing gate. Now keep hedge on L.-hand side and go ahead to a wooden stile leading into wood beside Knapp Farmhouse – where you will find violets, primrose, lesser celandine, red campion, bluebell, dog's mercury, wild garlic, ground ivy.

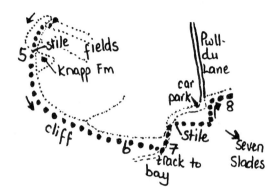

5. Keep on narrow path along top of wood (do not take path to R.). Path will emerge on top of cliff, giving stunning views over Pwlldu Bay and across to the Devon coast. Pwlldu ("black pool") Bay has a limestone pebble storm beach which forces the Bishopston stream to percolate its way onto the beach from a dammed pool. One of the buildings at Pwlldu was once the 18th century Beaufort Inn, with quite a smuggling history. Across the bay is Pwlldu Head, where there is evidence of its quarrying past. Beneath the E. slopes of the Head is "Gravesend", where are buried at least 68 press-ganged men who drowned when the "Caesar" was wrecked here in 1760.

6. Take the path on, until it dips to the broad track leading down to the bay. Look for stonechat, dunnock, warblers, skylark, green woodpecker, heron and cormorant. (Turn R. if you wish to visit the bay – path goes down to the houses, crossing a bridge and passing between the houses to reach the beach).

7. Turn L. onto the track and branch off up steps to stile on R. just before you reach the small car park. Cross over, and walk onto headland for the views. Look E., to see good examples of raised beach across "Seven Slades".

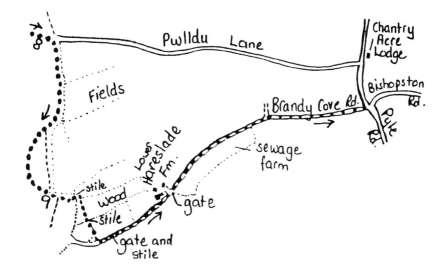

8. (A quick return to Pyle Corner can be made by following the lane out of the car park.) The walk continues east along the clifftop above Seven Slades. Where the path divides, take the R.-hand path nearer the sea. It rounds the headland giving views across Caswell Bay to White-shell Point. Flowers here include: dunesfoot cranesbill, silverweed, yarrow, hairy bittercress and common rockrose. As you continue, Brandy Cove – the next bay below the headland – is seen, with sand at low tide.

9. Leave the headland on the path which drops through scrub (do not take vertical path on R.) to a fence with stile and dog-gate at top of wood. Take the stepped path R. down through the wood to a stile. Go ahead from stile (note excavations showing the area's mining past) to leave by another stile and then ahead 6m to a path. (Turn R. to explore the beach at Brandy Cove – smuggling past!).

10. Turn L., go ahead over stile beside wooden gate (do not take path on R.) uphill on track. Pass Lower Hareslade Farm on L., go through metal gate and continue up lane (bush vetch, greater stitchwort, goose-grass, garlic mustard, wild strawberry.) At the sewage works, the lane becomes metalled, and continues to Brandy Cove Road and Pyle Corner.

51

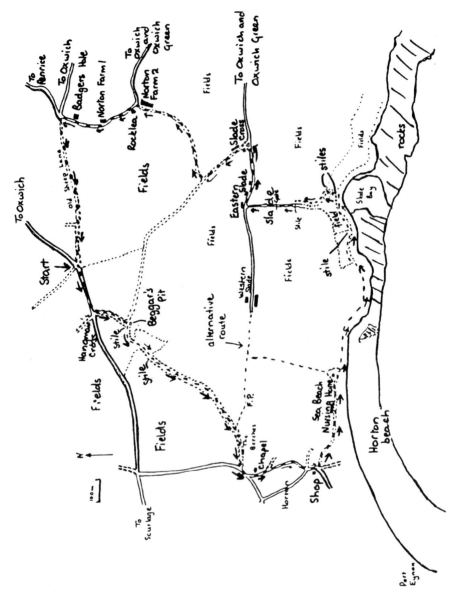

Walk 11, general map

52

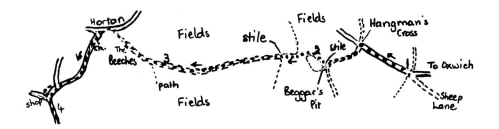

11. Hangman's Cross to Old Sheep Lane, via Horton and Slade

Length: 5.5 km (3.5 miles)   *Time: 2.5 hrs*

1. Start at the junction of the green lanes on the road between Oxwich and Horton (Grid ref: 484868). Take the road west, towards Horton and at Hangman's Cross (in 250m) turn L. down a wide track. Where this bends sharply L. at Beggar's Pit, cross stile on R. into field.

2. Go ahead and 2 signs point the way, following first the line of hawthorns, and then the hedge on the R. Cross the stile to continue along a path between hedges.

3. In 750m, the path widens; 30m beyond this point, bear R. and on reaching the road, turn L. downhill. Take the first turn on the L. and continue downhill, past a road junction and turn L. into an access lane just beyond the shop (fennel, red valerian).

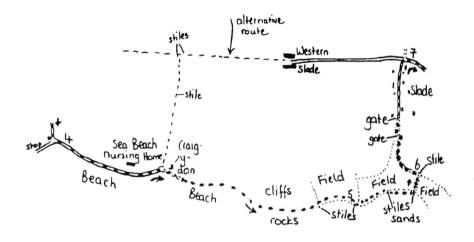

4.   Continue to the end of the lane, passing the Sea Beach Nursing Home. Take the narrow path to the R. of "Craig y Don", signposted "Oxwich". The path goes above the rocks and sea at the base of the cliffs. (Look for tree mallow, bloody cranesbill, rock rose, milkwort; buzzard, raven and linnet.) Cross the stone stile, and continue on the seaward side of the fence.

NOTE: This section of cliff is subject to continual erosion and care should be exercised at all times. The path is occasionally closed owing to cliff erosion and the recommended alternative route is to cross the stile near "Craig y Don" and go N. uphill crossing 2 stiles until a transverse path is reached. Turn R. and continue through Westernslade Farm and along the farm access road until the road junction at Pt. 7 is reached.

5.   At the second field boundary, ignore the path to the L. and cross the stile. Slade Bay now comes into view. Continue along the clifftop to the end of the field. In front of the next stile, turn L. to walk up the edge of the field, with the hedge on your R.

6.   Cross the stile and turn L. along a track (note wild mignonette) that widens and becomes grassy as it bends uphill to the R. Continue uphill, through the kissing gate and follow the metalled road between the houses of Slade to the T-junction.

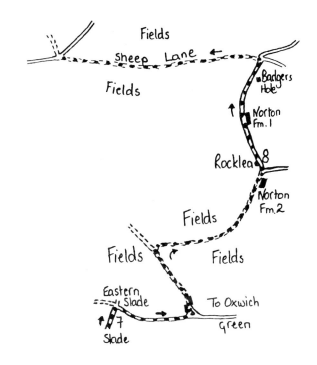

7.   Turn R. and go along the road until you reach the triangle of grass with a seat on the L. (climbing corydalis). Turn L. here, to walk between houses onto a broad track. Take the green lane on the R. in 250m and follow this down to Norton.

8.   At the road, turn L. and continue past Norton Farm and Badgers Hole on the R. (ramping fumitory). Where the road to Oxwich is sign-posted descending to the R., take the narrow path on the L. (S.P. "Berry 2.4 km"). This bridleway is known as Old Sheep Lane and is a fine example of an old Gower highway, cobbled in parts. It gradually climbs between high banks and where it opens into a wider tractor track, continue ahead to the start of the walk. This latter part of the walk offers good views across to Cefn Bryn.

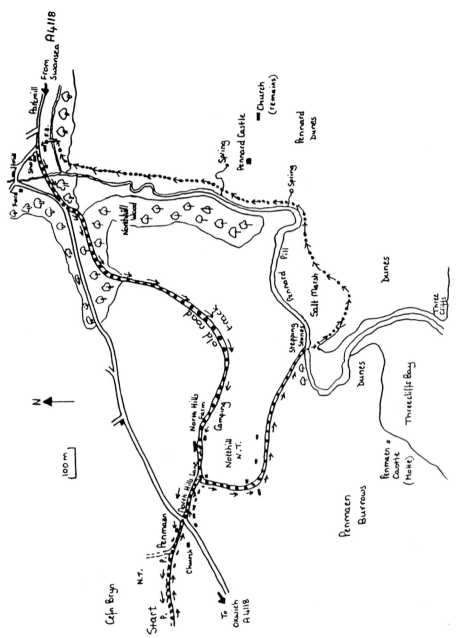

Walk 12, general map

56

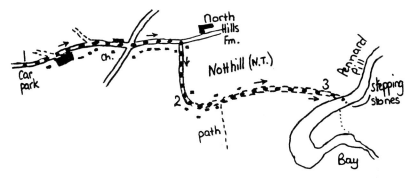

12. Penmaen, Notthill and Parkmill

Length: 4.5 km (3 miles)   *Time: 2 hrs*

This walk starts from the picnic site at the foot of Cefn Bryn, 400m
past the church on the minor road which semi-circles the north of
Penmaen village (Grid ref: 529888). In wet weather, parts of the walk
may be muddy. On a high Spring tide, the valley may be flooded so
that it is impossible to cross the stepping stones.

1.   From the picnic site, there are good views S. over Three Cliffs
Bay. Walk down the road to the main S. Gower road, near the church
of St. John the Baptist. Cross over onto a metalled road (North Hills
Lane). Pass houses on R., and after about 100m, turn R. along a
metalled track leading downhill. On the L., rise the slopes of N.T.-
owned Notthill (= North Hill).

2.   As the track swings L. and downhill, its surface becomes rougher.
In front, there opens out a wide view of Three Cliffs Bay. The slopes of
Penmaen Burrows rise on the R., crowned at the end by the remains of
Penmaen Castle (an early Norman defensive ringwork).

3.   Continue to the base of the track and onto the sandy-shingle edge
of Pennard Pill. It is not unusual to see a heron here, or waders in
profusion, feeding between this point and the meanders to the sea
(redshank, dunlin, knot, oystercatcher, various gulls). The limestone
points of the "Three Cliffs" have been considerably eroded this century.
There is a hollow arch through the base of the cliffs. The dunes below
Penmaen Castle are a cause for concern, as they are very unstable
and may disappear completely. Cross over the stepping stones onto the
opposite bank.

4.   Looking up the valley you can see the ruins of Pennard Castle high on the R.-hand side. This was built in the late 13th century, but much of it has collapsed. It was besanded and abandoned by 1650.

5.   Walk towards the far side of the valley, following roughly the line of the shingle-sand bar (an inner storm bank). This avoids the damper area where salt-tolerant plants abound, e.g. thrift, sea plantain, sea purslane, sea lavender, sea spurrey, sea poa, sea aster. Buzzard and kestrel are often seen; also wood pigeon and green woodpecker in Northill Wood on the L. Possibility of kingfisher on the stream.

6.   Follow the valley upwards towards Parkmill. You can make the steep climb up to explore Pennard Castle ruins, and the chapel nearby which was also besanded, probably about the mid 16th century. On the walls of the castle grows Draba aizoides (yellow whitlow grass), found here, and on only a few other places in Gower – and nowhere else in the country. It flowers from February to April with tiny clusters of yellow flowers.

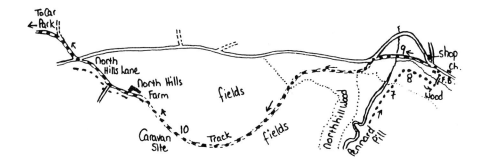

7. As the stream nears Parkmill, there is a considerable damp area (on the L.) which supports clumps of marsh marigold in Spring and, later, purple loosestrife and meadowsweet. Follow the path through the scrub/woodland and look out for long-tailed tits.

8. Continue above the stream (on your L.) through the wood. The path drops down to the water. Cross the footbridge and follow the narrow path 40m to the main road. (Beware, traffic!). There is a General Stores here in the village of Parkmill. Turn L. along the road. On the R., can be seen the buildings of the old water-driven mill, which gives Parkmill its name. The mill-wheel is still in place.

9. Go along the main road, about 250m. Opposite the road to Parc le Breos, turn L. down track through a gateway. Take the clear track that winds uphill through Northill Wood. This track was the original road, before the new road was cut through in the first part of the last century (wild garlic, bluebell, wood anemone, dog's mercury, nuthatch, tree-creeper, woodpeckers, tits). At the top of the wood, the track continues between farm field banks. The banks support many other flowers, including greater stitchwort, violets, red campion, primrose, wild straw-berry, lesser celandine, honeysuckle, goosegrass, garlic mustard.

10. The track passes, on the L., the North Hills Farm caravan site. Pass through the farmyard and into North Hills Lane. Cross the main road into Penmaen and continue up the minor road to the picnic site.

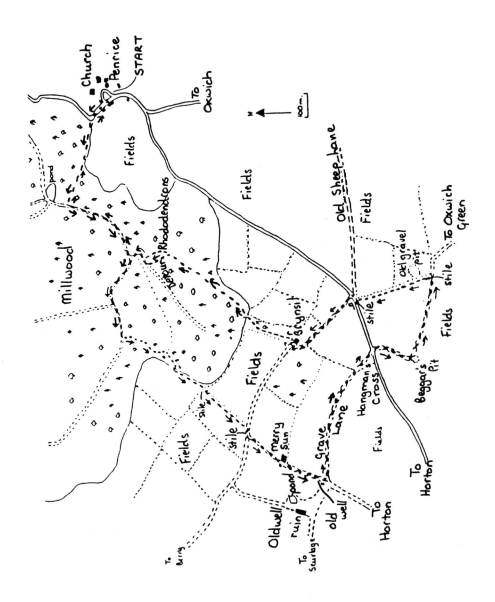

Walk 13, general map

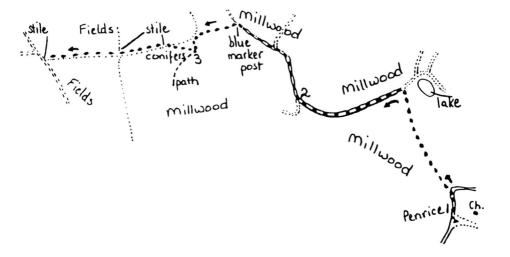

13. Penrice, Millwood, Grave Lane and Brynsil

Length: 7.5 km (5 miles)   *Time: 3 hrs*

1. Start from the village green in Penrice (Grid ref: 493879) and go downhill on the road (R.). At the bend, in 50m, turn L., taking a path dropping downhill through the woods following a valley. At the bottom, turn L. onto a wide gravel track that climbs upwards. (Look for woodpeckers and tits.)

2. At a bend, turn R., following the track until you take the L. branch at another bend. Continue ahead until you see a narrow path leading into the woods on the L., by a blue marker post. Take this narrow path crossing the ditch, and continue through the wood until 10m past the 4th blue marker post.

3. Turn R. to enter the conifers and follow the poorly defined path, leftish, until you emerge at the wood edge by a stile. Cross the stile and turn L. to go up the edge of the field and ahead up the second field (buzzard, kestrel; field pansy, corn spurrey).

61

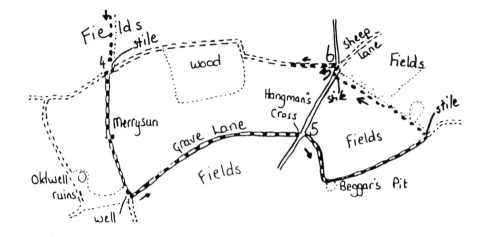

4. Pass over the stile, turn R. and in 10m take the green path to the L. between hedges. You will pass the renovated cottage called Merrysun. Continue and take the first L. turn, to follow the broad track known as Grave Lane, appropriately, since it brings you to the road between Oxwich and Horton at Hangman's Cross.

5. Cross the road taking the track opposite (very wet in winter). In 200m the track bends sharp L. Note the large hole on the R., known as Beggar's Pit. Continue along the lane and at the end of the L.-hand field, go over the stile on the L. Go ahead alongside the hedge and cross the stile onto the road. Turn R. along the road for 20m until a track crosses.

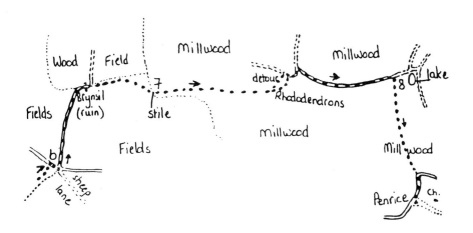

6. Turn L. and take the wide track. As it bends, you pass the ruin of Brynsil. Enter the field on the R. immediately beyond the house and follow the L.-hand hedge down towards the wood. Halfway down, head to the R. a little, aiming for the stile that leads into Millwood (pheasant; common fumitory).

7. Cross the stile into the wood and take the path ahead. Keep ahead and ignore any side paths. If the path near the rhododendron bushes is too wet, it can be avoided by a detour to the L. Both the detour and the original path emerge onto a broad gravel path. Turn R., and R. again to follow the track down until you are almost at the lake.

8. Turning R. you climb out of the wood by the path you followed at the start of the walk. At the road, turn R. and go uphill to Penrice and your starting point.

Other books published by the Gower Society
(and in print in 1999)

A Guide to Gower   Don Strawbridge, Peter J. Thomas (eds.)
Plant Life in Gower   Gordon Goodman
The Sea beneath My Feet   J. Mansel Thomas
The Gower Yarns of Cyril Gwynn
Gower – the journal of the Gower Society, published annually since 1948

Some further reading

Berney, J., 1985, *A Guide to Gower: the Seashore*. Culver House Press
Davis, P. R., 1997, *Historic Gower*. Christopher Davies
Douglas-Jones, P., 1997, *Three Corners of Gower*. D. W. Jones (Printers) Ltd.
Edmunds, G., 1979, *The Gower Coast*. Regional Publications
Gillham, M. E., 1977, *The Natural History of Gower*. D. Brown & Sons Ltd.
Grenfell, H. E., 1985, *Gower Images*. Culver House Press
Grenfell H. & Morris, B., *The Castles of Gower*
Grenfell H. & Morris, B., *The Caves of Gower*
Grenfell H. & Toft, L., *Noteworthy Gower Churches*
Holt, H., 1996, *Pwlldu Remembered*
Lucas, R., 1984, *A Gower Family*. The Book Guild Ltd.
Lucas, R., 1989, *Rhossili: a Village Background*. D. Brown & Sons Ltd.
Lucas R., 1998, *Reynoldston*
Morris, B., 1998, *Old Gower Farmhouses and their Families*. The Gower Society
Orrin, G. R., 1979, *The Gower Churches*. The Rural Deanery of West Gower
Rees, D. (ed.), 1977, *A Gower Anthology*. Christopher Davies
Thomas, J. M., 1982, *Yesterday's Gower*. Gomer Press
Vaughan-Thomas, W., 1976, *Portrait of Gower*. Robert Hale
Williams, G. (ed.), 1990, *Swansea: an Illustrated History*. Christopher Davies

Gower Society Membership

For details, send a stamped, addressed envelope to the Membership Secretary, The Gower Society, c/o Swansea Museum, Victoria Road, Swansea SA1 1SN.